Little Book of
FLORAL DESIGNS
FOR SILK RIBBON
Helen Dafter

SALLY MILNER PUBLISHING
(MILNER CRAFT SERIES)

First published in 2000 by
Sally Milner Publishing Pty Ltd
PO Box 2104
Bowral NSW 2576
Australia

© Helen Dafter, 2000

Designed by Anna Warren, Warren Ventures, Sydney
Photography by Sergio Santos
Printed and bound in China

National Library of Australia
Cataloguing-in-Publication Data

    Dafter, Helen.
        Little book of floral designs for silk ribbon.

        Includes index.
        ISBN 1 86351 2640.

        1. Silk ribbon embroidery. 2. Ribbon work. 3. Ribbon flowers. I. Title.
        (Series: Milner craft series).

        746.44

List of Flowers

$\mathcal{B}$asic $\mathcal{R}$equirements

SCISSORS

Sharp embroidery scissors are a must, keep them with your work and use them only for the ribbons and threads, this way they will stay nice and sharp.

EMBROIDERY HOOP

Use an embroidery hoop at all times. Choose one large enough to surround the entire design thus avoiding bruised stitches. By using a hoop the tension is maintained on the embroidery fabric leaving you to concentrate on the tension applied to the stitching.

NEEDLES

Always use a chenille needle for the silk ribbon. Nos. 18, 20 - 24 are the sizes I most frequently use depending on the width of the ribbon I am working with. The correct size needle will protect the edges of the ribbon by forcing the fibres of the fabric apart to allow the easy passage of the ribbon through the fabric.

AS GENERAL RULE:

7 mm ribbon — Size 18 chenille needle
4 mm ribbon — Size 18 – 20 chenille needle
2 mm ribbon — Size 22 – 24 chenille needle

FABRIC

Fabric choice is almost unlimited in woven fabrics ie cotton, silk and wool. Some of the lighter fabrics might require a bonded interfacing to stabilise them prior to embroidery. Knitted fabrics are generally more difficult to work on.

STRANDED THREADS

Rajmahal stranded art silk threads have been used exclusively in the flower designs for detail stitching, colours simply matched to the silks where required. The lustre of this thread compliments the silk ribbon perfectly. Rajmahal threads are identified by number throughout. One strand is used at all times unless noted. (DMC threads could be substituted if desired).

A No. 9 crewel needle is used for the Rajmahal thread.

SILK RIBBONS

Plain coloured silk ribbons have been used extensively for the flower designs, but overdyed or variegated silk ribbons have been incorporated in several of the flower designs {detailed as (0)} to demonstrate how effective the subtle shade variations are when used in silk ribbon embroidery. Silks are identified by number (where applicable) and a personal colour description. The width of the ribbon used is also noted.

If desired you could substitute different colours for those used as many of the flowers illustrated are available in a vast range of colours and shadings. The colours I have chosen to work with are merely a suggestion, you might like to use a different to personalise your work.

MARKING PENS

I use a water erasable pen, to mark in the stem lines or the flower centres before to beginning the embroidery. Any visible marks can be simply removed using a cotton bud dipped in cold water and allowing the embroidery to air dry.

TRANSFERRING DESIGNS

There are several methods for transferring designs, depending on your fabric choice.

Designs can be transferred onto light fabrics:

• Simply by drawing on freehand

• By enlarging or reducing the designs for these flowers and using a light box (or sunny window) as a light source and placing the fabric over the design sheet and following the lines (through the fabric) with a fabric marking pen.

Woollen fabric (such as a cot or pram blanket):

• Draw the designs freehand

• Use a piece of fine tulle to transfer the design. Simply place a piece of greaseproof paper between the tulle and the design. (This will protect the design drawing). Use a permanent marking pen to draw over the stem lines or flower centres, wait for this pen to dry. Place the tulle over the blanketing and using a fine water erasable marking pen to redraw over the lines on the tulle allowing the pen tip to penetrate the tulle. This will give a reasonable indication of stem positions and flower centres. If the lines are very faint simply draw over them once the tulle is removed.

PAINTED BACKGROUNDS

Painted backgrounds have become a recognisable feature in many of my embroidery designs and they are used here to create additional dimension and interest for each of the flower designs. A painted background is not essential for this type of embroidery to be successful, but it does give you the opportunity to create an impression of added depth to the completed embroidery. I use acrylic folk art paint, in very limited colour ranges to paint the background fabrics. All the backgrounds for the flower designs in this book were created using one colour only, green, mixed with water (to create a wash consistency) before it was applied using a bristle brush to dry fabric. If you are working on a project which will need occasional laundering, for example, a cushion or baby's blanket, the addition of textile medium to the paint (mixed according to the manufacturers directions) prior to diluting and applying the paint will ensure the paint, once dry, is permanent.

DESIGN CREATIVITY

The flowers shown here will give you enormous scope to create many different design combinations for ribbon embroidered projects. They can be simply one flower or a combination of as many as you like to work. Do try and draw some of the stems freehand, if you persevere you will find new freedom in your embroidery and will soon be able to place flowers where you want them and be able to create unique projects and gifts for yourself or appreciative friends.

HELPFUL HINTS FOR THE FLOWER DESIGNS

• The component parts for each flower group have been listed in the order in which I have worked them.

• French knots are used extensively for flower centres and clusters, they are one wrap French knots unless otherwise noted.

• The combination of stitches used to form a flower bud is shown in the stitch guide which starts on page 42.

• The photographs of the flower designs are shown actual size. The drawings have also been kept to scale. The scale of the flowers can be increased or decreased slightly, depending on the position and combination in which you choose to work, by making your stitches smaller or larger. You can also use different width ribbons to alter the size of the flowers you create.

• A tiny spider web has become a recognisable trademark in my designs and is to be found once again amongst the flowers in this book. It is created using one strand only of Madeira metallic machine sewing thread (silver) and straight stitches only. The spider is a one wrap French knot in Rajmahal 29, Charcoal.

$\mathcal{A}$GAPANTHUS

THREADS
421 Green Earth

RIBBONS
20 Medium grass green 4mm silk
125 Light blue 2mm silk

Leaves
Extended and couched
ribbon stitch in 20.

Flower petals
Ribbon stitch in 125.

Stems
Stem stitch / straight stitch
in 421 thread.

AUTUMN LEAVES

THREADS
841 Gilded bronze

RIBBONS
(0) Petals/Autumn Leaves 4mm silk
77 Terracotta 4mm silk

Stems
Stem stitch in 841
thread.

Leaves
Ribbon stitch in (0).
Ribbon stitch in 77.

$\mathscr{C}$ARNATIONS

THREADS
926 Verdigris

RIBBONS
127 Light raspberry pink 2mm silk
5 Very pale pink 2mm silk
32 Light blue green 2mm silk

Stems
Stem stitch in 926 thread.

Flowers
Petals — Ribbon stitch in
127 & 5.

Buds
Ribbon stitch in 127 & 5.

Leaves
Ribbon stitch in 32.

Bud calyx
Ribbon stitch in 32.

$\mathcal{C}$INERARIAS

THREADS
521 Maidenhair

RIBBONS
1 Antique white 4mm silk
118 Deep blue mauve 4mm silk
102 Deep mauve 4mm silk
145 Fuchsia pink 4mm silk
72 Dark jungle green 7mm silk

Stems
Stem stitch in 521 thread.

Flowers
Centres — French knot in 1.
Petals — Ribbon stitch in 118,
102 & 145.

Leaves
Ribbon stitch in 72.

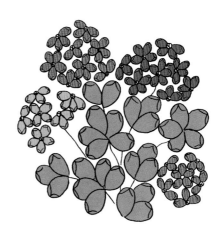

$\mathcal{C}$LIVEA

THREADS
521 Maidenhair
94 Moroccan gold

RIBBONS
72 Dark jungle green 4mm silk
106 Tangerine 4mm silk

Leaves
Extended / couched ribbon
stitch in 72.

Stems
Stem stitch in 521 thread.

Flowers
Petals — Ribbon stitch in 106.

Bud detail
Pistil stitch in 94 thread.

$\mathscr{C}$YCLAMEN

THREADS
926 Verdigris

RIBBONS
128 Raspberry pink 4mm silk
157 Very light dusky pink 4mm silk
33 Medium blue green 7mm silk

Stems
Stem stitch in 926 thread.

Flowers
Centres — French knots in 128.
Petals — Ribbon stitch in 157.

Bud details
Fly stitch / straight stitch in 926 thread.

Leaves
Ribbon stitch in 33.

Leaf detail
Straight stitch in 926 thread.

$\mathcal{D}$AFFODILS & JONQUILS

THREADS
805 Sassafras

RIBBONS (DAFFODILS)
33 Medium blue green 2mm silk
15 Bright yellow 4mm silk
13 Pale lemon 2mm silk

RIBBONS (JONQUILS)
33 Medium blue green 2mm silk
16 Orange 4mm silk
15 Bright yellow 2mm silk

Leaves (Daffodils and Jonquils)
Extended / couched ribbon stitch in 33.

Flowers (Daffodils)
Trumpet — Loop stitch in 15.
Petals — Ribbon stitch in 13.

Flowers (Jonquils)
Centres — French knot in 16.
Petals — Ribbon stitch in 15.

Buds (Daffodils and Jonquils)
Ribbon stitch in 15.

Stems (Daffodils and Jonquils)
Straight stitch in 805 thread.

Bud detail (Daffodils and Jonquils)
Fly stitch / straight stitch in 805 thread.

$\mathcal{D}$AHLIAS

THREADS
521 Maidenhair

RIBBONS
130 Deep burgundy 4mm silk
50 Rich deep red 2mm silk
20 Medium grass green 4mm silk

Stems
Stem stitch in 521 thread.

Flowers
Centres — French knots
(1 wrap) in 130.
Petals — Ribbon stitch in 50.

Buds
French knots (2 wrap) in 130.

Bud detail
Fly stitch in 521 thread.

Leaves
Ribbon stitch in 20.

$\mathcal{D}$UTCH HYACINTHS & PANSIES

THREADS (DUTCH HYACINTHS)
Ecru
521 Maidenhair

RIBBONS (DUTCH HYACINTHS)
72 Dark jungle green 4mm silk
14 Pale yellow 4mm silk

THREADS (PANSIES)
Ecru
521 Maidenhair

RIBBONS (PANSIES)
15 Bright yellow 4mm silk
178 Light grape 7mm silk
85 Deep purple 7mm silk
2 Black 4mm silk
20 Medium grass green 2mm silk
20 Medium grass green 7mm silk

Dutch Hyacinths
Leaves
Extended / couched ribbon stitch in 72.

Stems
Stem stitch in 521 thread.

Flowers
French knots in 14.

Pansies
Flowers
Centres — French knot in 15.
Petals — Ribbon stitch in 178 & 85.

Upper petals — Ribbon stitch in 2.
Detail — Straight stitch in Ecru thread.

Buds
Ribbon stitch in 178 & 85.

Bud calyx
Ribbon stitch in 2mm 20.

Stems / details
Straight stitch in 521 thread.

Leaves
Ribbon stitch in 7mm 20.

Leaf detail
Straight stitch in 521 thread.

$\mathcal{F}$REESIAS & LILY OF THE VALLEY

THREADS (FREESIAS)
521 Maidenhair

THREADS (LILY OF THE VALLEY)
65 Laurel green

RIBBONS (FREESIAS)
20 Medium grass green 2mm silk
12 Clotted cream 4mm silk

RIBBONS (LILY OF THE VALLEY)
21 Dark forest green 4mm silk
3 White 4mm silk

Freesias
Stems
Stem stitch in 521 thread.

Leaves
Extended / ribbon stitch in 20.

Flowers
Ribbon stitch / French knot
in 12.

Lily of the Valley

Stems
Stem stitch in 65 thread.

Leaves
Extended / couched ribbon stitch
in 21.

Flowers
French knots in 3.

GARDENIAS

THREADS
521 Maidenhair

RIBBONS
3 White 4mm silk
21 Dark forest green 4mm silk

Stems
Stem stitch in 521 thread.

Flowers
Ribbon stitch (7 of) in 3.

Buds
Ribbon stitch in 3.

Bud calyx
Side ribbon stitch in 21.

Leaves
Ribbon stitch in 21.

$\mathcal{G}$LADIOLUS

THREADS
926 Verdigris

RIBBONS
74 Smokey grey green 4mm silk
(0) Glenlorin 'Sarah' 4mm silk

Leaves
Extended / couched ribbon
stitch in 74.

Stems
Stem stitch in 926 thread.

Flowers / buds
Ribbon stitch in (0).

Flower detail
Straight stitch in Ecru.

Bud detail
Straight stitch in 926 thread.

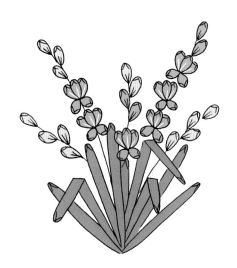

$\mathcal{I}$CELAND POPPIES

THREADS
926 Verdigris
841 Gilded bronze

RIBBONS
172 Light mango 4mm silk
13 Pale lemon 4mm silk
156 Dark cream 4mm silk
33 Medium blue green 2mm silk

Stems
Stem stitch in 926 thread.

Flowers
Centres — French knots (2 wrap) in 841 thread.
Petals — Ribbon stitch in 172, 13 & 156.

Buds
Ribbon stitch in 172, 13 & 156.

Leaves
Ribbon stitch in 33.

Bud calyx
Ribbon stitch in 33.

$\mathcal{L}$ILLIUMS

THREADS
521 Maidenhair
Ecru
243 Grape
171 Woodlands

RIBBONS
1 Antique white 4mm silk
163 Very light rose pink 4mm silk
20 Medium grass green 4mm silk

Stems
Stem stitch in 521 thread.

Flowers
Lower petals — Ribbon stitch in 1
Upper petals — Ribbon stitch in
163.

Buds
Ribbon stitch in 1 & 163.

Bud detail
Fly / straight stitch in 521 thread.

Leaves
Ribbon stitch in 20.

Petal detail
French knots in 243 thread.

Stamens
Stem stitch in Ecru thread.

Anther
Straight stitch in 171 thread.

$\mathcal{N}$ASTURTIUMS

THREADS
521 Maidenhair

RIBBONS
13 Pale lemon 4mm silk
(0) Glenlorin 'Sandstone' 4mm silk
20 Medium grass green 7mm silk

Stems
Stem stitch in 521 thread.

Flowers
Centres — French knots in 13.
Petals — Ribbon stitch in (0).

Buds
Ribbon stitch in (0).

Bud detail / spur
Fly stitch / straight stitch in 521
thread.

Leaves
Ribbon stitch in 20.

Leaf detail
Pistil stitch in 521 thread.

$\mathscr{P}$RIMULA & TULIPS

THREADS (PRIMULA)
521 Maidenhair

THREADS (TULIPS)
521 Maidenhair

RIBBONS (PRIMULA)
128 Raspberry pink 4mm silk
20 Medium grass green 4mm silk

RIBBONS (TULIPS)
72 Dark jungle green 4mm silk
15 Bright yellow 4mm silk
156 Dark cream 4mm silk
50 Rich deep red 4mm silk

Primula
Stems
Stem stitch /straight
stitch in 521 thread.

Flowers
French knots in 128.

Leaves
Ribbon stitch in 20.

Tulips
Stems
Stem stitch in 521 thread.

Leaves
Extended / couched ribbon
stitch in 72.

Flowers
Ribbon stitch in 15, 156
& 50.

$\mathscr{S}$UNFLOWERS

THREADS
521 Maidenhair

RIBBONS
67 Medium brown 4mm silk
15 Bright yellow 4mm silk
20 Medium grass green 7mm silk

Stems
Stem stitch in 521 thread.

Flowers
Centres — French knots in 67.
Petals — Ribbon stitch in 15.

Leaves
Ribbon stitch in 20.

Stitch Glossary

RIBBON STITCH

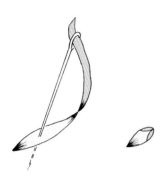

Draw the ribbon through the fabric, using the shaft of the needle along the length of ribbon to ensure that the ribbon is laying flat against the fabric. Put the point of the needle through the ribbon 8–10mm from the start and gently pull the ribbon back through itself until the ribbon forms a gentle petal-like point.

EXTENDED RIBBON STITCH

Formed in the same way as ribbon stitch, but the stitch is worked in varying lengths as required.

COUCHED RIBBON STITCH

Often worked in conjunction with extended ribbon stitch to create the strap like foliage of different flower groups. Start the stitch as you would for basic ribbon stitch, determine the length required and hold the ribbon flat against the fabric. Two or three small stitches in a complimentary colour of stranded thread are worked across the width of ribbon to 'couch' this in place on the surface.

The ribbon is then folded over these stitches, hiding them from view and the ribbon stitch is completed in the method described above.

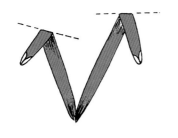

FRENCH KNOT

Draw the ribbon through the fabric. With the needle facing away from the fabric, twist the ribbon around the needle, stand the needle upright and put the point of the needle back into the fabric close to where it emerged. Before pulling the needle and ribbon through to the back of the fabric pull the ribbon quite tight to tighten the wrap on the needle. Pull the needle through to the back of the work. (By applying tension to the ribbon before pulling the needle through to the back of the fabric you ensure even sized french knots)

Spider web or woven rose

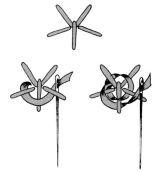

Using two strands of a thread in the same colour as the ribbon chosen for the rose work the 5 spokes of the 'web'. The spokes must be an even length and evenly spaced. Anchor this thread off securely. Draw the ribbon through the fabric at the centre of one of the segments. Reverse the needle and simply weave the eye of the needle with the ribbon attached under and over the spokes alternatively. Allow each subsequent round of ribbon to sit next to the one before it, avoid pulling too tightly as this will create a bulky rose. Allow the ribbon to twist and fold as you weave and this will create a very natural looking rose. Return the ribbon to the back of the work and fasten off.

Stem stitch

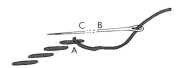

This stitch is most often worked in stranded thread to create the stems and branches of the various flowers. Begin at A, reinsert at B and emerge at C, repeat the process until stem is desired length and shape.

Straight stitch

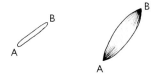

Most often used to create flower details or stems using stranded thread. Begin at A, insert at B, fasten off or move to the start of the next stitch.

FLY STITCH

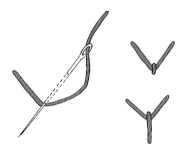

Draw thread through fabric at A, reinsert at B, emerge at C. The resulting 'V' is held in place by reinserting the needle and taking a small holding stitch through the fabric. This holding stitch can also be lengthened to create the stem of a bud.

COMBINATION OF STITCHES TO FORM FLOWER 'BUDS'

Flower buds or partially opened flowers are formed using a combination of stitches in both ribbon and thread.

1. A single bud = 1 ribbon stitch + 1 fly stitch + 1 straight stitch

2. A larger bud = 2 ribbon stitches + 1 fly stitch + 2 straight stitches

3. Partial flower = 3 ribbon stitches + 1 fly stitch + 3 straight stitches

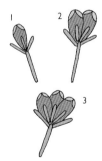

Silk Ribbons

	mm	2	4	7
1	antique white		★	
2	black		★	
3	white		★	
5	very pale pink	★		
12	clotted cream		★	
13	pale lemon	★	★	
14	pale yellow		★	
15	bright yellow	★	★	
16	orange		★	
20	medium grass green	★	★	★
21	dark forest green		★	
32	light blue green	★		
33	medium blue green	★		★
50	rich deep red	★	★	
67	medium brown		★	
72	dark jungle green		★	★

	mm	2	4	7
74	smokey grey green	★		
77	terracotta	★		
85	deep purple			★
102	deep mauve		★	
106	tangerine		★	
118	deep blue mauve		★	
125	light blue	★		
127	light raspberry pink	★		
128	raspberry pink		★	
130	deep burgundy		★	
145	fuchsia pink		★	
156	dark cream		★	
157	very light dusky pink		★	
163	very light rose pink		★	
172	light mango		★	
178	light grape			★

Overdyed Ribbons

Autumn leaves	4 mm	(Petals brand)
Sarah	4 mm	(Glenlorin brand)
Sandstone	4 mm	(Glenlorin brand)

Rajmahal Stranded Art Silk Threads

521	Maidenhair	94	Moroccan Gold	171	Woodlands
841	Gilded Bronze	805	Sassafras	65	Laurel Green
926	Verdigris	243	Grape		Ecru

STOCKISTS

Most of the Stockists listed below are the wholesalers or the Australian distributors or manufacturers. If you have any difficulty obtaining any of the threads which I have used, the Stockists listed below will be able to advise you of the closest retail outlet.

1. RAJMAHAL STRANDED ART SILK
   Rajmahal
   1 Anderson Street
   Bendigo Vic
   Australia 3551

Phone   03 5441 7787,
Fax   02 5441 7959

2. YLI SILK
   Cotton On Creations
   PO Box 804
   Epping NSW
   Australia 2121

Phone   02 9868 4583,
Fax   02 9868 4269

3. OVERDYED SILK
a) Petals Australia
    PO Box 5357
    Nambour Qld
    Australia, 4560

Phone   07 5441 5797,
Fax   07 5441 5697

b) Glenlorin
    PO Box 974
    Pennant Hills NSW
    Australia 1715

Phone   02 9980 1993

ACKNOWLEDGEMENTS

My thanks once again to Sally Milner Publishing for keeping faith and giving me another embroidering opportunity. This second volume of embroidered silk ribbon flowers has given me an excuse to visit one of my favourite places — my garden, to study flower forms and colours and once again interpret these in silk ribbon for fellow embroiderers to follow. This volume has expanded considerably the range of flowers which I can now use to create 'garden' embroideries or simply use just one flower sample to embellish a gift or create a small individual project

Thank you also to many friends and students, your encouragement, laughter and support keep me sane along the way.

Finally, my thanks to Glenn, Naomi, Matthew and Brian, my family, for showing patience and giving me the space to be creative, your love and support makes all the difference.

HELEN DAFTER 2000